INSIDE the inbetweeners

An Unofficial Guide

charlotte wilson

joe thomas

simon bird

blake
harrison

james buckley

the inbetweeners'
magic formula

Who'd have thought four semi-geeky, averagely sex-obsessed, awkward, potty-mouthed sixth-formers would become the nation's pin-ups? *The Inbetweeners* is the personal disaster diary of posh kid Will McKenzie as he roughs it at Rudge Park Comprehensive, and shares his misadventures with mates Simon, Jay and Neil.

The Inbetweeners' true-to-life comedy crosses generations, from teenagers to thirtysomethings – there are even tales of grandmas nearly falling off their chairs with laughter. Most of us have experienced the kind of teen angst that afflicts the boys, and amidst the hail of crude, cringing and hilarious jokes you'll also find truly touching moments. The show has picked up armfuls of awards, and with the film and US version of the show, it's heading towards global geek domination.

All this has meant sudden stardom for young actors Simon Bird, Joe Thomas, James Buckley and Blake Harrison. Admittedly not always the greatest with girls in their own teen years, they now have millions of fans, and people shouting out *Inbetweeners* catchphrases to them in the street – "clunge", "bus wankers", that kind of thing. The secret formula of their screen chemistry, they say, is farts and hugs. Thanks, boys.

So here it is – your (unofficial) inside guide to the lewdicrously funny world of *The Inbetweeners*. Schooldays, huh? Who'd wanna go back there?

1

who are the inbetweeners?

Somewhere between the cool kids and the nerds lurk the "inbetweeners". Never quite getting in with the hottest girls. Never quite managing to be seen in the right places. Will McKenzie, Simon Cooper, Jay Cartwright and Neil Sutherland – posh and know-it-all, lovesick and moody, mouthy and filthy-minded, dim but nice apart from the smells – are the *Inbetweeners* at Rudge Park suburban Comprehensive.

Then there are the girls they lust after – Carli, Charlotte and Tara (and Will's mum, of course). And the teachers and families who seem to exist only to make their lives more difficult and even more embarrassing.

We all know an "inbetweener" – because that's us up there on the screen: our measly, cringey, boring, stupidly funny adolescence revealed.

aka Briefcase Mong

Will McKENZIE

played by Simon Bird

Ponce

6

The inside report

Will came to the sixth form at Rudge Park from a private school, where his mother says he was bullied – but according to Will, it was only a couple of wedgies. Immediately shunned and abused for his briefcase, clumpy shoes and posh voice, he quickly found his social level – very near the bottom, and completely uncool.

Will is more academic than his friends, but prone to uncensored shouting fits at inappropriate times (in front of parents, teachers, disabled people). He can be cuttingly funny and would like to be teacher's pet, which is a shame as he's clearly an object of disdain for Mr Gilbert, the head of sixth form.

It is unanimously agreed, except on Will's part, that his mum is well fit. However, any suggestion that his friends date or wank over her is met with mortified outrage by Will. The situation probably isn't helped by Mrs McKenzie's apparent over-protectiveness, or her occasional and seemingly needless forays into the living room whenever Jay, Simon or Neil are round.

Will is always putting himself forward for things – like organizing the school prom, or reinventing himself and friends as cool London clubbers, or hiring a boat. Very occasionally it comes off, but usually it ends in humiliation, or someone risking hypothermia in Swanage harbour.

Will and Charlotte

- For some unimaginable reason, Charlotte Hinchcliffe, one of the hottest girls in school, seems to like Will. The others all think she must be doing it for a bet, or to get back at her ex, Mark Donovan.

- According to actor Simon Bird, Will's dream date with Charlotte would be to go to the theatre in London, followed by a bar, dinner and a walk along the Thames before going back to a hotel – all with her totally naked.

- So is Charlotte keeping Will dangling, or does she really like him? Series 3, episode 1 gives perhaps the clearest explanation of her feelings about Will.

Personal highs:

- Charlotte consenting to have sex with him.
- Modelling in the fashion show (with Charlotte).
- Being asked personally by Mr Gilbert to head the Duke of Edinburgh's Award.
- Organizing the school's Christmas prom – and it being a success, apart from that incident with Neil and Miss Timbs.

Personal lows:

- Not actually managing to have sex with Charlotte.
- Finding French exchange student Patrice in bed with Charlotte.
- Loudly abusing a group of young people with learning disabilities at Thorpe Park.
- Soiling himself in his exams – and everyone in school knowing.
- Being thrown off the Duke of Edinburgh's Award through no fault of his own (Jay's sick wanking was to blame).

7

Vrooom

aka Boner

POO!

Simon COOPER

8

played by Joe Thomas

The inside report

Simon Cooper – indecisive, moody, hopelessly romantic and possibly, at a push, almost good-looking. Unfortunately for Simon this asset doesn't seem to be backed up by self-belief or the ability to think for himself. He's a hostage to his besottedness with Carli D'Amato, and held back by two things: his parents and his mates.

His mum and dad's overt sex life is shoved in his face at every opportunity, and perhaps it's this that renders him useless at the act himself. That and his mates' frankly nonsensical advice. Simon's life is a series of frustrations. If it weren't for his even-less-successful friends, he could be seriously depressed. As opposed to mildly depressed.

Temperamental and shouty, Simon's sulks often result in minor tantrums. Like a little boy who can't ever seem to get his own way, he has been known to stage a sit-down protest on the roof of the family shed. Worse – much worse – he has resorted to ranting like a psychopath at his malfunctioning penis at crucial moments. Like when he was finally in bed with the gorgeous Tara.

Perhaps Simon's only hope is his parents' decision to relocate to Swansea. Who knows, without his misguided mates on hand to ruin everything for him, Simon might actually find true happiness with a member of the opposite sex. But then again, who would tell him what to do?

Personal highs:

- Passing his driving test.
- Carli kissing him when he helps with her Geography revision.
- Getting a real Valentine's card – even if it is from Hannah Fields in the year below.
- Carli asking him to model for the school charity fashion show.
- Meeting a fit girl (Tara) who isn't Carli and who wants to have sex with him.

Personal lows:

- Finding out that the car his dad has bought him is truly tragic.
- Any time that Carli's on-off boyfriend Tom is around.
- Throwing up over Carli's little brother.
- Leaving his left bollock hanging out at the fashion show.
- His old chap letting him down just as he's about to lose his virginity.

Simon and Carli

- Simon has been in love with Carli since they were eight. He realizes this in a flash when he bunks off school and gets drunk – and lets the whole suburb know about it by spray-painting her drive. In the face of repeated rejection by his beloved, he continues, like a wasp ramming its body against glass, to woo the only girl he has ever loved. Ever will love. Ever could love…

- The idea of playing hard to get is an alien concept. It appears he'll do anything – from shelving his own exam revision to helping Carli nail longshore drift, to wearing tight Speedos on the school catwalk. And we all know how that one ends up.

Bangin!

Jay CARTWRIGHT

played by James Buckley

10

The inside report

Potty-mouthed Jay has some of the most unforgettable and hilariously pornographic lines in the show. He has almost single-handedly ensured that the word "clunge" is heading for inclusion in the *Oxford English Dictionary*.

Jay never misses an opportunity to insult his mates. His common target is Will, his polar opposite in practically every way, though Simon and Neil don't get off lightly either. But what lies behind Jay's persistent vulgarity? Perhaps the answer is close to home... Jay's even fouler-mouthed dad.

From outing his son as a cushion-shagger to repeatedly humiliating him in front of his friends, Mr Cartwright is the bane of poor Jay's life, and surely the one responsible for his fictional sexual anecdotes. If it weren't for the family dog Benjy (RIP) poor old Jay would have no one to turn to with the truth about his sad, girlfriendless existence.

His tall tales are legendary. According to Jay, he was trialled for West Ham, phoned by Ralph Lauren, took a driving course when he was ten, and has apparently got to Africa in a pedalo with a mate. Supposedly his photographic memory means he doesn't have to do exam revision – and the teachers say it would be unfair on the other kids.

Personal highs:

- Going for football trials at West Ham.
- Sex with a Dutch girl – well horny.
- But really... Managing to save face by scoring actual drugs at a gig.
- Going out with Chloe.
- Getting to have a wank in an old people's home.

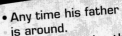

Personal lows:

- Any time his father is around.
- His father having their dog Benjy put down.
- Scoring tea from Mark Donovan, and having to pretend it's dope.
- ~~Being dumped by~~ Dumping Chloe.
- Getting caught having a wank in an old people's home.

Jay and Chloe

- After he gets talking to grammar-school girl Chloe at the bus stop, Jay has a character transformation. He won't hear a crude word about her, and when the others ask, he doesn't deny that he loves her.

- But his devoted texting and jealous checking on her all the time are too much for Chloe – who says she isn't ready for someone so needy. His mates rally round a tearful Jay, and no one's allowed to mention the subject. But if anyone asks, he had to dump her because she's frigid, and he was just too well-endowed.

HELP!
phoarr!
Neil SUTHERLAND
played by Blake Harrison
ouch!
LAGER

The inside report

Tall, dim and with serious flatulence issues, Neil is always several beats behind his friends. On the plus side, he's not bad-looking and has a winning party piece: robotic dancing – a spectacle both embarrassing and admirable in equal measure. If Neil didn't keep saying stupid things he'd be a catch.

With his extreme dim-wittedness, it doesn't seem to cross Neil's mind to worry about whether or not girls fancy him. He just goes for it, taking rejection in his stride – unlike his neurotic sidekicks.

For similar reasons, Neil is oblivious to his dad's blatant campness. According to Neil, his mum left because she was in a difficult place, not because his dad wears eye-wateringly skimpy shorts.

At least Neil is the only one with a job. In fact, his role as Mr Monkey at Thorpe Park gets his mates in free. Although they aren't quite so pleased when wasps fly inside his suit and Neil strips it off – to reveal he's butt-naked underneath.

Poor Neil... placid, unambitious, and just a bit thick, it's his kind heart that will get him through in life. Even if his rare violent outbursts (punching a fish to death?) are really quite worrying when you think about it...

Neil's surprising conquests

- Where the others score a gruesome zero, Neil quietly triumphs. It's Neil who wins the race to have actual full sex – rather than Jay's imaginary orgies, Will's technique disaster, or Simon's equipment failure.

- He's a relative winner in the world of work, too. The local newspaper doesn't want to swap him for Will, because he's the best work experience placement they've ever had. But he is also a magnet for the attentions of school "paedo" Mr Kennedy.

- Neil even snogged Charlotte Hinchcliffe – and though he swears to Will it was only a snog, his grin suggests he got something more.

Personal lows:

- Will never getting him a date with Mrs McKenzie.
- Not being able to drive a plane on his work experience.
- Mr Gilbert dragging him away just when he was in with Miss Timbs at the school prom.
- Projectile pissing – on himself and Will – when they share a bed in Warwick.
- Getting a motorbike for his birthday, then watching helplessly as Jay destroys it.

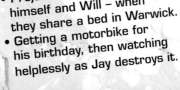

Personal highs:

- Getting a blow job – or several – from Kerry after his eighteenth (though he admitted she was still crying a bit during the first one).
- Finding a pair of Mrs McKenzie's worn knickers in the wash basket.
- Bonding with new drinking soulmates at Warwick University.
- Discovering he hasn't got a woman pregnant – it's just chlamydia.

Glamourista

15

ATLAS

Carli D'AMATO

played by Emily Head

14

The inside report

Carli is an alpha female at school. Clever, pretty and idolized by Simon. She has a gaggle of mates who tag along behind her, and even when she's being moany she reels in the male attention. It's Carli who organizes the school charity fashion show – and gets to hand out the choice modelling jobs.

Carli and Simon's parents are friends, and the two have known each other since childhood. Sometimes she babysits her little brother, and one evening she asks Simon round when her parents are out – after he spray-paints a heart on her drive. Simon has spent most of his life pining for Carli, but it always seems as though he's her "last resort" – or comes in handy when she needs a favour... Mind you, she does choose Simon as her emergency fashion show partner.

She's into older men, anyway. Her boyfriend Tom is a totally fit rugby player. Her friends think Simon's a sad case, and Simon's friends think Carli's a tease – and it ain't never gonna happen between them.

So is Carli just using Simon? She does give him a snog after he sabotages his own exam chances to help with her Geography. He might just be in with a chance – if he didn't screw up every opportunity he has with her.

Personal highs:

- Simon Cooper declaring his love for everyone to see – on her parents' driveway.
- Simon being such a star helping with her revision.
- Getting back with Tom.
- Organizing the school fashion show.
- Simon agreeing to model for it – and having a great body.

Personal lows:

- Simon puking up over her little brother.
- Will being a mean little twat with his so-called moral objections to the fashion show.
- Tom going off with his rugby mates.
- Simon wrecking her fashion show moment – it wasn't funny for Carli.

Carli and Tom

- He's older. He doesn't need fake ID to be served in a pub. He plays rugby. And his car isn't a sad little yellow poncemobile with one red door.

- Whenever Carli and Tom's on-off relationship is back on, Simon doesn't stand a chance. Carli gets all menstrual when Tom opts to see his infantile rugby mates instead of her, and in the last episode of series 2 she tells Simon that they've split up. But it's just another opportunity for Simon to make a dick of himself – because by the time exams have finished, Carli and Tom are so predictably back together.

Flowers - urgh!

aka BIG Jugs

Spurt!

FIZZ

>>>>>>>>

Charlotte HINCHCLIFFE

played by Emily Atack

in the works

16

The inside report

Georgeous, blonde Charlotte is something of a mystery – or perhaps it's just the way *Inbetweeners* creators Damon Beesley and Iain Morris have written her. With a *Nuts* pin-up figure, she's definitely an alpha, like Carli, but with something of the free spirit about her. Charlotte's presence at a party makes it instantly cool.

Charlotte and Will bond over a bottle of contraband champagne, and from that point on Will is smitten. But he never knows where he is with Rudge Park's resident Jessica Rabbit. She seems to blow hot and cold. Drawn to Will's slicing wit, she's clearly physically way out of his league. Much to Will's indignation, Charlotte prefers to date the likes of the mindless Mark Donovan, though she does invite Will round for some casual sex – with humiliating results for Will.

Charlotte's in the year above the boys, and by series 3 she's off at uni – returning only for the school fashion show and to fulfil Will's mum's warning about pretty girls. Gentle and fragile (according to Donovan) she can also seem cruelly unthinking about Will's feelings – though, to be fair, he also brags immaturely about her as a conquest.

The big question is... Did Charlotte really munch off the whole rugby team?

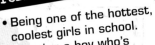

Personal highs:

- Being one of the hottest, coolest girls in school.
- Meeting a boy who's really kind to her – though obviously he couldn't be her actual boyfriend.
- Doing some modelling for a catalogue.
- Going to university.
- Being invited back to Rudge Park as a "special guest" for the school charity fashion show.

Personal lows:

- Mark Donovan still tagging around.
- Will being completely useless in bed and a virgin.
- Being called Big Jugs – does no one realize she has feelings?
- Getting a bit lonely at university.
- Wanting to go out with a boy who's kind to her, but not finding anyone suitable.

Will's other crush

- Will also manages to mess things up with new girl Lauren Harris on the school field trip. Partly because he seems to think two hours of Yoda impressions are a guaranteed chat-up technique, and partly because he has a better-looking mate.

- Will just won't accept that Lauren fancies Simon, and hangs around cringingly in the background – even when she invites Simon to join her for their free time and they share a goodbye nuzzle. It's almost pistols at dawn as Will and Simon out-sneak each other in the battle for Lauren's attentions. All of this leading to the infamous Swanage boat rescue. Luckily, she has to move away soon after.

Emo!

Screamo!

BEEP!
BEEP!
BEEP!

Watch
the
fringe
man!

Tara

played by Hannah Tointon

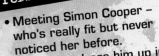
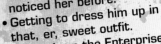

The inside report

With grungy T-shirts and streaks in her hair, Tara fancies herself as an indie emo kid – like she'd just die without Spotify. Undeniably Tara is hot... So hot, in fact, that she knocks Carli D'Amato off her throne as Queen of Simon's Heart.

Tara is confident, sexually curious and seems genuinely into Simon. She organizes a weekend away so they can both lose their virginity. (Though she probably didn't count on his mates coming, too.)

There is the odd gross moment with Tara – she sees nothing wrong with vomiting then snogging Simon's face off, and her attempt to matchmake Will with her friend Kerry is misguided to say the least.

She does also want to make Simon her personal shopping project. Much to his mates' amusement and Simon's horror, she persuades him to try a ridiculous pink cardigan, bow tie and shorts by saying how much she fancies him in them – then gets him to model them at Neil's tragic eighteenth birthday party.

But even laid-back Tara draws a line somewhere. And when Simon starts going mental and shouting at his penis in the throes of what should be a very special moment, he definitely crosses that line. Shame, because they made such a lovely couple.

Personal highs:

- Meeting Simon Cooper – who's really fit but never noticed her before.
- Getting to dress him up in that, er, sweet outfit.
- Going down the Enterprise to see bands.
- Kissing Simon at a Failsafe gig – and he didn't seem to mind the vom.
- Managing to arrange a trip to stay with her sister at Warwick so they can have sex.

Personal lows:

- Simon's saddo mates hanging around all the time.
- Will dumping Tara's friend Kerry – and after Kerry's dad died recently, too.
- Simon's friends hijacking their romantic Warwick weekend.
- Simon scaring her with his outburst at his penis.
- Having ever met Simon.

When Tara meets Simon

- Tara first catches Simon's eye when he's literally running after Carli – and falls back into Tara's lap in the sixth-form common room. She's in the year below, and explains that he probably hasn't noticed her before because she's just dyed her hair and grown tits.

- She's reading the *NME*, and declaring in a muso-geek way how it's wrong about everything. Simon's so obviously bluffing when he says he loves music, too. The last (and first) gig he went to was Take That, with his mum. But Tara lets him invite himself to see Failsafe with her at the Enterprise.

oooh...

MILF

...crrr!

Mrs McKENZIE
played by Belinda Stewart-Wilson

20

The inside report

Polly McKenzie is the MILF of the series. Slim and vivacious, with a cascade of dark curls, she's every teenage boy's fantasy and the subject of all Will's friends' wet dreams. She's not like other mums. Oh no. Will's mum looks sexy on the school run.

Obviously Will is far too old to be driven to school, but Mrs McKenzie is either over-protective or guilt-ridden, because she insists – and now Will has to suffer all manner of coarse innuendo from his mates on a daily basis.

Mrs McKenzie appears oblivious to any real problems Will has – "Mummy's boy" issues, perhaps? She seems blind to his physical limitations, too. Any fool could see that a tight CK vest would make him look like a circus act rather than a member of JLS, but not Mrs McKenzie. If only she were more encouraging about his romantic prospects. Warning him to aim lower than a girl like Charlotte is harsh. (She's right, obviously.)

Mrs M seems oblivious to her own charms, except when the raw Gallic sexuality of French exchange student Patrice has her giggling like a schoolgirl, much to Will's utter disgust. But when she goes on a rare weekend away with a man of her own age, Will doesn't like this either.

Mrs McKenzie and her Petal

- Will's mum treats him like a child. She calls him "Petal" and is always revealing squirmy details to his friends. Like that he cried on the Ghost Train (although Will points out that he was only five).

- She reminds him about his asthma, and gives Neil full instructions on how to deal with Will's migraines (there are suppositories in the bathroom, and Neil will have to put them up Will's bottom).

- But when Will swallows dope at the gig in series 3, episode 2, it's his mummy he wants. Because he thinks he's in a bubble, everything is going flat, his hands are sausages, and he's worried he might be dead.

Personal highs:

- Going to see INXS for her first gig, and one of the band skateboarding on stage.
- Simon's French exchange student Patrice being so gorgeous and charming.
- Finding her old school flame Fergus on Facebook.
- Going away with Fergus for the weekend.
- Will not getting into too much trouble – so they don't have to move school again.

Personal lows:

- Will's father leaving them.
- Having to move because Will was bullied at his old school.
- Will's friend Neil trying to be her friend on Facebook.
- Fergus dumping her because he says he can't be dealing with a "problem child".
- Rather a lot being spent on her Ocado account while she was away.

Mr GILBERT

played by Greg Davies

The inside report

He's terminally grumpy, grudgingly world-weary and, at six feet eight inches, towers over the Rudge Park sixth formers like a vindictive giant. Mr Gilbert appears to take great pleasure in making life difficult for his students and seems to delight in their small misfortunes.

The head of sixth form doesn't even try to disguise his contempt – especially when it comes to that annoying busybody/grass/toffee-nosed Will McKenzie. But could it be that Gilbert sees in sharp-but-hapless Will a reflection of his own younger self?

Gilbert's personal life is largely a closed book – but he says he is single, and maybe he really does fancy Will's mum Polly, while making out that it's a joke at Will's expense.

Chinks of humanity also glimmer through his armour of harsh satire when Gilbert is seen choosing a cuddly toy, and he shows real kindness to "paedo" Mr Kennedy, removing him gently from temptation on more than one occasion.

Personal highs:

- No one at the school prom throwing their arms around him and saying that he's all right for a teacher.
- McKenzie and crew being thrown off the Duke of Edinburgh's Award.
- The end of the school year – and not having to see any sixth-formers for a glorious six weeks.

Personal lows:

- Being spotted by Sutherland and Cartwright choosing a cuddly toy at Waterside.
- Having to drag Mr Kennedy away from Sutherland – again – at the fashion show.
- The beginning of a new term.

Ideas to improve school

Sprung!

In real life

Greg Davies, who plays Mr Gilbert, was himself a teacher for many years. He's an award-winning stand-up comedian and in line to host his own TV show. He has also appeared on *Mock the Week* and *Never Mind the Buzzcocks*. Or you could catch him on the National Grid's Facebook page, giving advice about gas leaks and carbon monoxide to students.

Neil's DAD
played by Alex MacQueen

The inside report

Kevin Sutherland is a long-suffering single father, looking after Neil and sister Katie. Their house even smells poor, according to the boys. For Neil's eighteenth birthday all his father manages as a present is a small family party at home – while Neil's mum buys him a brand new motorbike.

Everyone is convinced that Kevin is gay. The evidence? His taste in shorts, and that he only goes out on a Wednesday evening – and then it's to play badminton. With another man. Even the other parents think Kevin is gay, despite Neil's exasperated protestations.

In real life

You may recognise Alex MacQueen (not to be confused with the late fashion designer Alexander McQueen) from his long-running *Holby City* role as anaesthetist Keith Greene. Or as Julius from *The Thick of It*.

Neil's SISTER
played by Kacey Barnfield

The inside report

It's Neil's sister versus Will's mum in the "who would you rather shag?" debate. Youth and pertness versus experience and huge boobs is how the boys reckon it.

Older sis Katie tends to appear without many clothes, opening the door to greet the boys in a slinky robe. But she is clearly off-limits and out of their league. She has taken on some of the motherly tasks, though – it's Katie who's ironing Kevin Sutherland's trousers when everyone arrives for Neil's eighteenth. Katie's live-in boyfriend works in a garage, but is no help with fixing Simon's car door.

In real life

Before Kacey Barnfield gained tabloid fame by dating England cricket star Stuart Broad, she was much better known as *Grange Hill* bully Maddie Gilks. Her family has an estate agency business in Enfield, north London.

Jay's FAMILY

played by
David Schaal and Victoria Willing

The inside report

With his toxic toilet smells, retch-worthy bodily noises and terrible sense of pee direction, Terry Cartwright is not someone to share a room with for long. He's a bully, undermining his son at every opportunity with his sadistic tirades, and probably laying into his mother, too. No wonder it sounds like Jay had to see a shrink when he was younger.

We rarely see Mrs Cartwright, except when she makes tea for the boys in the family caravan at Camber Sands. Although she does have a tendency to walk in on Jay at potentially embarrassing moments – like when he's trying to stash his porn mag in a Scalextric box, or having a wank.

The family dog Benjy (apparently a mixed-breed terrier) comes to a tragic end in Home Alone – and has inspired his own online fan page and unofficial T-shirt.

In real life

Victoria Willing (Jay's mum), co-wrote *Could It Be Forever?*, a theatre show about having a teenage crush on David Cassidy. David Schaal (Jay's dad) was Taffy the warehouse manager in *The Office*.

Simon's FAMILY

played by
Martin Trenaman, Robin Weaver and Dominic Applewhite

The inside report

Simon is constantly being embarrassed by the rest of the Coopers – mother Pamela, obnoxious little brother Andrew and especially his father Alan. Andrew is almost certainly brighter than Simon and thinks his brother's crush on Carli is tragic (but then, so do most people).

Simon's father is always giving too much information about where and how often he and his mother have had sex. In series 2 episode 5 he briefly leaves Pamela, who sobs her way through Will's mum's barbecue – something Simon finds incredibly irritating and is completely unsympathetic about.

In real life

Robin Weaver, who plays Simon's mum, has appeared as four different characters in episodes of *Casualty* over the years.

KAMA SUTRA
FOR PARENTS

Patrice

played by Vladimir Consigny

The inside report

Patrice's appeal is a mystery to the *Inbetweener* boys. He smokes, he talks about sex all the time, and he pees in the street. And he doesn't take the hint, either. When the boys run away from him to gatecrash a party he just saunters along behind them.

Peeoux!

But Patrice does have his uses. With his smouldering eyes, leather jacket and scent of manliness he's, well... so French. Patrice charms Will's mum and effortlessly wangles VIP party treatment. But then Will finds him in bed with Charlotte and... ouch.

In real life

Vladimir Consigny, who plays Patrice, appears as the son of his real-life mother Anne Consigny in the French film *Wild Grass*.

Mark DONOVAN

played by Henry Lloyd-Hughes

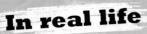

The inside report

Right from the start, psycho Rudge Park bully Mark Donovan is out to stab, throttle or otherwise violently assault Will. And that's even before Will gets off with Charlotte Hinchcliffe, who is Donovan's ex. He likes a bit of puff, and occasionally manhandles Will - but never actually follows through on his direst threats.

He's sweet and polite to parents - especially Will's mum - and perhaps does have a sensitive side, coming over all quietly protective when he finds Will and Charlotte in bed. Mind you, he does issue a promise of death at the same time.

In real life

Henry Lloyd-Hughes is the actor behind Mark Donovan. He appeared in *Harry Potter and the Goblet of Fire* as Ravenclaw Quidditch captain Roger Davies.

25

Which Inbetweener are you most like?

1. You're going on a date with a girl way out of your league. What's your plan of action?
a) Bore her to death with your A-level revision notes.
b) Invite all your mates along for moral support.
c) Get her in the mood with your rampant sex anecdotes.
d) Express your feelings through the medium of dance.

2. A relative died and left you £500. What would you do?
a) Put it in a high-interest savings account for your university fees.
b) Spend some on new golf shoes, and the rest on shit clothes that you feel a total twat in but that your hot girlfriend insists make you look lush.
c) Tell everyone you've got a great investment tip from Lord Sugar, but secretly blow the lot phoning sex-line numbers.
d) Buy something stretchy and shiny and comfortable to dance in from the costume-hire shop in town.

3. Which university do you plan to go to?
a) Oxbridge, of course.
b) Er, it would depend where your crush since childhood was going.
c) University is for virgins. Who wants to spend valuable muff time learning and doing exams?
d) Warwick looks well wicked, with all those rugby blokes and drinking games.

4. You're having a party – what are your essential ingredients?
a) Witty conversation, canapés and vintage mineral water.
b) The girl you've loved since she was eight.
c) Wall-to-wall clunge and a box of Ribbed for Her Pleasure.
d) Two litres of orangeade.

26

5. You're under age – what do you do to try and get served in a pub?
a) Study the small print of the drinking laws to find a way round them.
b) Steal the contents of your dad's drinks cabinet instead.
c) Confidently present a fake ID, but have to put on an accent to fit the country it's from.
d) Go to the wrong one.

6. Where would you escape to on holiday?
a) A secluded spot in the great outdoors to commune with the beauties of nature.
b) Somewhere romantic for two – maybe Paris?
c) Caravan Club – it's like a mobile orgy.
d) Why would I want to escape? Are you sending me to prison? I didn't do nothing...

7. You've been invited to a girl's house, but you've got the runs. How do you deal with it?
a) Explain about your sensitive stomach and find a seat near the toilet.
b) Take some Immodium and hope for the best – you'd rather die than admit you have bodily functions.
c) Try and get it all out in one sitting as soon as you get there, then blame the appalling smell on the dog or the dodgy plumbing.
d) Feel totally relaxed about passing wind in front of her – everyone farts all the time at your house.

8. If you were head of sixth form for a day, what would you change?
a) You already have a list of a hundred ways you could improve how the school is run – if only they'd listen to you.
b) You're not very good at being authoritative – you'd probably get one of your mates to make any important decisions.
c) Make it school law that all the girls come to school naked and up for it.
d) Nah, that's too creepy – turning into someone else for a day.

So who are you?

Mostly a)
Sensible, superior – perhaps a bit of a geek? Come on, admit your Will tendencies and embrace the inner nerd. Let's hope you've got the wit and endearing weaknesses to make you entertaining and not too unbearable.

Mostly b)
Romantic, sensitive (relatively speaking, that is) and easily led – are you a Simon? Perhaps it's time to grow some balls and take control of your own life. Just don't leave them hanging out of your pants in public.

Mostly c)
Do you ever think of anything other than sex? Or perhaps, like Jay, you're bigging yourself and your conquests up to hide your insecurities. If you want a real girlfriend, you may have to let down your guard. And start trademarking those corkers now.

Mostly d)
Hello? Anyone there? You probably know already that you're not the sharpest tool in the box. But remember that Neil's generally liked, and gets a lot more action than the others. Although you may want to get those bowels checked out.

Chapter 2

How did it get here?

Before it exploded on to our screens in all its genius humour, *The Inbetweeners* was a brewing notion in the minds of writers Iain Morris and Damon Beesley. But how did these two men in their thirties manage to make the show so true to teenage life? And how did they wrangle it on to TV?

Now *The Inbetweeners* has squillions of fans and a bag-full of awards, and is set to follow *The Office* and *Skins* across the Atlantic.

Remind yourself what you missed – and love – in each episode of the three full series.

Damon Beesley and Iain Morris

Iain Morris

Born
Damon Beesley: 1971, suburban London.
Iain Morris: 1973, Woking, Surrey.

Education
Damon Beesley didn't go to university, but worked in magazine publishing instead. Iain Morris studied theology at Bristol University.

How they met
Working in the late 1990s on Channel 4's *The 11 O'Clock Show*, which launched the TV careers of Sacha Baron Cohen and Ricky Gervais. Beesley and Morris set up Bwark Productions together in 2004.

Pre-tweeners careers
Beesley was a commissioning editor for E4 and also produced comedy at Ealing Studios. Morris co-hosted Jimmy Carr's XFM radio show and appeared in the spoof TV documentary series *Look Around You*. He worked as a commissioning editor at Channel 4, bringing us *Phoenix Nights*. Perhaps his greatest achievement (bar *The Inbetweeners*) was being script editor for several years on *Peep Show*.

| 0 | 1 | 2 | 3 | 4 | 5 | 6 |

New   Save   Delete   Word count   Print

≫ Document-The Inbetweeners ≫ Modified-10.02.2011 ≫ Format-MASSIVE

Damon Beesley

Fans of...
Graham Linehan, writer of Father Ted. Also US films American Pie and Ferris Bueller's Day Off.

Iain Morris thinks Fawlty Towers is the best sitcom ever – you can see the Basil Fawlty influence when Simon shouts at his equipment.

Other comedy creations

Beesley and Morris wrote two episodes of *Flight of the Conchords* (The Actor in season 1 and Unnatural Love in season 2).

The Inbetweeners are born

We have Beesley's and Morris's former girlfriends to thank for *The Inbetweeners*. They dumped the two of them around the same time, and the pair moved into a seventh-floor penthouse bachelor pad in central London. They spent their time on the PlayStation and mulling over the funny and tawdry tales of their misspent twenties and thirties – stories they started collecting in their "Anecdote File".

There's another woman to thank, too. When Morris decided to leave Channel 4 to try to write a script, his boss Caroline Leddy had the foresight and impeccably dodgy taste to commission his and Beesley's idea.

In the show's original pilot, James Buckley (now Jay) played Neil. The other three were cast afresh when the series finally got the green light.

Will is me?

Morris says he was something of a Will at school – and many of the things that happen to Will actually did happen to him. Including the conversation with his mum about migraines, the sliding backwards and forwards trying to have sex, and skidding around on the floor shown at the Caravan Club party. Although most of this happened at university and in his twenties – not his teens.

The Ricky Gervais connection

In the *Extras* episode with Patrick Stewart, Gervais's character Andy gives the *Star Trek* actor the sitcom script he has written, and it finds its way to the BBC. The comedy commissioning editors Andy goes to see there are called Iain Morris and Damon Beesley (although they are played by actors). Allegedy, the real Morris injured Ricky Gervais's back while they were wrestling in his front room.

The Flight of the Inbetweeners

The MTV version of *The Inbetweeners* in the US is being directed by *Flight of the Conchords* director Taika Waititi.

31

Everyone's an "inbetweener"

Inbetweeners creators Beesley and Morris figured that millions of people must have had a similar experience to their own teen years – growing up in suburbia and being pretty ordinary at school. And it looks like they were right. After the first six episodes the show was recommissioned, and a million viewers were discovering their "inbetweener" side at the start of series 2. The show's comedy relies on real experiences, so for the second series Beesley and Morris researched anecdotes from Greg Davies (Mr Gilbert), Simon Bird (Will) and Joe Thomas (Simon) – but haven't said which ones came from whom. Beesley has admitted that the incidents with the fish in the boat and the amorous moment at the under-age disco came from his own youth. By the end of series 3, the show was chalking up viewing figures of three million.

Ooh look at them getting all poshed up at the Baftas!

Sun, sea and maybe sex in Malia

Crete's answer to Ibiza is the setting for the *Inbetweeners* film, which sees the boys taking their first holiday abroad away from their parents. They're all set up for a sea of clunge, but will they get out of their depth?

The actors went to Malia in summer 2010, but kept getting mobbed by – surprise! – drunken fans. Joe Thomas (Simon) has said it ended up being mainly a fun short break playing pool and drinking champagne. The rest of the filming – including fans of the show coming along to be extras as clubbers – took place in early 2011.

You'll have to wait and see if the four actors get their dream cameo appearances – they'd like Ricky Gervais to play a bartender and Stephen Merchant to be a drug dealer trying to sell the boys Es.

Inbetweeners USA

There was US interest from early on, and MTV began filming a pilot in January 2011 in Orlando, Florida. The boys are played by Joey Pollari (seen in Disney's *Avalon High*), Bubba Lewis (*To Save a Life*), Zack Pearlman (in Will Ferrell-produced *The Virginity Hit*) and Mark L Young (*Big Love*). Alex Franka (*Unanswered Prayers*) is the American Carli.

It's been reported that Justin Bieber thinks the UK show is so funny he'd make himself free to do a cameo in a fourth series or film. Maybe a "Hollywood friend" for Jay?

The School NEWSLETTER SERIES 1 read all about it!

1.1 THE FIRST DAY

Sh*t Day One: Ends with a stab threat

Will McKenzie's first day at Rudge Park Comprehensive is a foretaste of what is to come. Sporting an abuse-magnet of a name badge, he starts as he means to go on by loudly speculating that Mr Gilbert, the head of sixth form, sucks the headmaster's balls. Pictures appear of Will (played by Simon Bird, above) on the toilet, posted by school bully Mark Donovan, and everyone quickly realizes it's social death to be seen with the new kid. Everyone but Simon Cooper, who has won the nickname "Boner" for the hard-on he got when all-time crush, Carli D'Amato, leaned forward to smell his aftershave. Simon invites Will along with his mates, potty-mouthed Jay and gormless Neil, to the traditional post-first-day pub visit. Obviously they go to the wrong pub, and Carli is with her older, more desirable boyfriend, Tom. Not content with a totally shit day at school, Will grasses up the under-age drinkers and ends up on Mark Donovan's "To Stab" list.

REPLAY MOMENT
Neil and Jay bulldoze a kid in the pub into answering "Lee Sharpe" on a video game. It's the wrong answer – twice.

1.2 BUNK OFF

The park's a good place to stare at girls – but not to throw your Frisbee at them. Especially if they're in a wheelchair. Will, Simon, Jay and Neil start the episode on the run from Mark Donovan, then decide to bunk off school. Simon does a ridiculous impression of his mum on the phone to Gilbert, Will dresses up in Simon's dad's suit to buy alcohol and they bundle round to Neil's house. Everyone thinks Neil's father is gay, and Neil can't find the stash of straight porn he swears his father has. Drunk on gin and Drambuie, they're caught out by Neil's dad arriving with a carpenter, and Will

Love: Will they ever get together?

goes into one of his rants – involving the words "lips", "bell end" and "closet". Simon (Joe Thomas, left) declares his love for Carli in spray paint on her drive and amazingly she invites him round that evening. With Will minding Carli's seven-year-old bro, Simon gets all macho and tells her to finger herself – then spews all over her brother.

REPLAY MOMENT
Will explains carefully to Carli's brother how his parents will be obliterated by a terrorist attack on London.

1.3 THORPE PARK

Wreck: Is this car even sadder?

As Will observes, boys who drive are much more attractive to girls than those who don't. So, as the oldest, it's up to Simon to pass his test. Which looks pretty unlikely, frankly, until his examiner, Tracey, turns up and seems easily swayed by nice eyes, a passable adolescent physique and a laid-back approach to her thigh-squeezing. Funnily enough, Simon passes. His prize from his parents? The saddest Fiat Cinquecento Hawaii (Special Edition) on the planet. The boys test it out with a trip to Thorpe Park, where Neil now works and can get them freebies and a gawp at girls' boobs on the rollercoasters. But in a car park incident, Jay gets the Fiat's door knocked off. Neil is terrorised by a wasp in his Mr Monkey costume, then Will insults some young people with learning disabilities on the Nemesis Inferno ride – and they take their revenge on Simon's forlorn car.

REPLAY MOMENT

Simon reverses into a car in his driving lesson. Instead of reporting it, the instructor shouts agitatedly to drive on.

1.4 WILL GETS A GIRLFRIEND

It's a suburban teen party, with the boys bored senseless on a sofa, discussing how, according to Jay, Charlotte Hinchcliffe (played by Emily Atack, below) has munched off the whole rugby team. When Charlotte turns up, the party instantly becomes cool and, astoundingly, she chooses Will and his deadpan humour over Jay and his Crazy Frog impressions. Simon spends the night stalking the girl he fancies, and Jay turns out to have a friend who isn't a loser, but who did trials with him at West Ham (allegedly). Will gets a snog and some hand foraging action – and another death threat

Hot and cool: Does Charlotte use Will?

from Mark Donovan. Invited to Charlotte's house the next Friday, Will fails to have sex with her – because rocking your whole body up and down doesn't really count. Neil and Simon wind Jay up so much about his football friend that he goes mental jumping on the guy's car bonnet. Will cries in his mother's lap after Charlotte seems to be taunting him in the charity "Blind Date". But at least he can go with Simon and Jay to watch Neil with his thirteen-year-old "date" – and her mum.

REPLAY MOMENT

The boys wondering if they should tell Will, who is upstairs with Charlotte, that Mark Donavan has arrived – and Jay grassing Will up instantly.

1.5 CARAVAN CLUB

Getting some: The first rule of...

Tied to a chair with a bin on his head – courtesy of Mark Donovan – Will debates the merits of chavvy Bluewater versus the supposed campsite orgy heaven of Camber Sands, where Jay (James Buckley, above) goes with his parents. Which should the boys head for on their trip? The caravans win, and on the motorway Simon pushes his tinny car up to a tonne. As they arrive, Becky, a girl from the campsite, chats Simon up by text. But before they can try their luck at the dance that evening, the boys have to endure Jay's father, with his explosive bowels and loud jibes about Jay's sexual inadequacy. Neil's happy enough doing his robot dance, but Will wimps out from the sexual demands of a punky-emo girl with red hair, and has his shoes stolen by children. On Jay's advice, Simon lures Becky outside, drops his trousers and reveals his already applied condom. Not surprisingly, she is repelled. Disaster all round. On the long drive home, the boys find the back seats are wet, and Neil cheerfully reveals that it's the result of his exploits with the punk girl.

REPLAY MOMENT
The boys arguing over whose responsibility it is to clean up the "spunkmobile".

1.6 THE XMAS PROM

Simon's dad knows just the place to hire a suit for the Christmas prom – except that all the velvet and ruffles are a bit too jazzy and, even worse, so ancient they could have been worn by Simon's father when he was... you know... with Simon's mum. Jay perks up when Will says they'll be handing out the drink vouchers – because that means they'll have the pick of the birds. Neil gives too much information about his lust for Miss Timbs, who teaches Biology, and Will bores them all with an endless meeting. On the night it actually turns out to be a good party, and people enjoy it. Jay almost opens up and embraces his sensitive side

Dancefloor: Neil gets amorous

with Big John, before a female Jay-alike loudmouths it out of him. Simon decides against declaring his love for Carli. And Neil (Blake Harrison, left) lunges at Miss Timbs while wearing a reveal-all (or nothing) glam-rock body suit. The whole school saves Will from a pasting by Donovan, and as the boys lie on the trampoline in the gym, an incredible thing happens – Jay admits he didn't in fact get a blowie behind the DJ decks.

REPLAY MOMENT

Jay's heart-to-heart with Big John.

SERIES 2

2.1 FIELD TRIP

It's the legendary Swanage field trip (see the real-life Swanage, below right) and Will's second term at Rudge Park. On the coach, Jay is thrown off the coveted back seats by Mark Donovan, and proceeds to make an utter tit of himself by gesticulating at a party of pensioners. Will lucks out when he gets a seat next to new girl Lauren Harris, and seems not to be f*cking it up. That is until they arrive and Lauren spots Simon. This, plus Will's Yoda impressions, mean that he's blown out and Simon gets to do the survey with Lauren. Meanwhile, Jay's out canvassing women shoppers about their transport choices – and sexual preferences. Creepy Mr Kennedy gives Neil some vodka in return for getting his kit off to go sea-dipping. Will stitches Simon up by telling Carli and Lauren about each other, then hires a boat to take advantage of Lauren now being free. Of course, Simon, Jay and Neil pile in and havoc follows, ending with Simon naked (except for a sock), a dead fish and a demented rescue operation. Jay never does find his Swanage MILF.

‹‹‹‹‹‹‹

REPLAY MOMENT
Jay asking an elderly woman at a seafront ice-cream stand if she can suck him off.

2.2 WORK EXPERIENCE

Valentine's Day, and apparently more possibilities for total humiliation. Strangely, Jay has a lot of cards in the same scrawly handwriting… But Simon has a real one from Hannah Fields in the year below, and Will's flowers to Charlotte win him an invite to meet her at the under-eighteens disco where she's doing the bar. The work experience placements get mixed up, so Neil heads off to Will's dream job on the local newspaper, while Will bundles in and starts insulting the mechanics at the garage. Which, unsurprisingly to everyone but Will, leads to him being thrown in the river in his underpants. Later, he brags about Charlotte going like a porn star. But mechanic Wolfy turns up at the disco and Charlotte pays Will back with a drink in the face. Simon is pounced on by Hannah Fields, who gives him vodka and an episode highlight – an overt public wank. Unfortunately, he also gets a kicking from a twelve-year-old who thinks Simon insulted him. The four mates resort to hiding in the toilets. Luckily, Will's mum can come and pick them up…

‹‹‹‹‹‹‹

REPLAY MOMENT
The boys' discomfort watching Simon being seen to at the disco – he will keep making eye contact.

2.3 WILL'S BIRTHDAY

Jay's nicked an invite to a party – but it's the same night as Will's seventeenth birthday bash. And Simon has his sex-obsessed, chain-smoking French exchange student Patrice hanging around. Will, meanwhile, is IMing Charlotte, who takes a special interest in Patrice, yet goes offline when Will invites her to his birthday dinner. On the day, Will's mother gives him a Calvin Klein vest then blackmails him into wearing it that evening, making him look a total knob. Will's attempt at a sophisticated dinner party is a disaster. Not a single girl is coming – except the stripper Neil and Jay have booked. The only answer is to head to Louise Graham's party. Simon tries to invite some girls in the street, but they call him a paedo, and the boys can't even outrun Patrice to ditch him. At the party, Will gets dog shit on his jacket, forcing him to strip to his CK vest and endure ridicule. To top it off, he finds Patrice in bed with Charlotte. But at least it's Patrice and not Will that Mark Donovan is out to kill this time.

＜＜＜＜＜

REPLAY MOMENT

Jay's desperate attempts to close his laptop – almost impossible, as he's been giving himself a "Sleeping Beauty".

2.4 A NIGHT OUT IN LONDON

Will decides it's time the gang reinvent themselves as cool London clubbers. Carli and friend Rachel (who seems to like Will) even agree to come clubbing with them. Saturday, and Jay sorts through his condom drawer, before Neil reveals he can't take them because his car doesn't have an engine. On the way in Simon's Fiat they insult people at bus stops, but two Londoners catch up with them at the traffic lights and wring a pathetic "Sorry" from Simon. At the club, Simon is barred because he's wearing trainers. Solution: he swaps them for a homeless guy's shoes. It's not until Carli and her friend talk about the rank toilet smell following them around that Simon admits the shoes are drenched in tramp-piss. Will gets the cold shoulder from Rachel, who's with Dean, and Neil's accident on the way there – involving peeing into an empty can – means he keeps making dodgy groaning noises in the toilets and gets thrown out. Simon's car has been clamped, and he has to ring his dad…

＜＜＜＜＜

REPLAY MOMENT

A toss-up between Simon's sordid transaction with the tramp and Neil's painful penis in the club toilets.

2.5 DUKE OF EDINBURGH

Will is asked to organize the Duke of Edinburgh's Award scheme, while, in the common room, Neil and Jay are highly amused by a bloke online who's had half his hair removed with Immac. Simon and Neil think the Award will be all abseiling and whitewater rafting, but when Will runs into his old babysitter, Daisy, at his mum's barbecue, he has one of his brainwaves: Daisy is pretty, possesses a nurse's uniform and works at a local old people's home – a perfect DOE assignment. Despite the smells and incontinence, lust-struck Will offers to cover Daisy's all-night shift in return for a date, but has to bribe Jay to stand in for Simon, whose dad has left home and wants to bond. Just before his date, Will falls asleep, and Neil and Jay take advantage with the Immac. Panicked at his sudden nether hair loss, Will stuffs an old lady's wig down his pants and tries desperately to fend off Daisy's alcohol-induced attentions. Back at the home, Jay's quest for fresh porn material takes him squarely into O-A-Paedo territory, as he ends up wanking in front of an old woman.

REPLAY MOMENT
Jay's magnificent OAP wank.

2.6 END OF TERM

Exam time, and perhaps the boys' luck has changed. Carli invites herself to revise at Simon's house, and Jay is snogging a real-life, non-imaginary girl. Will, however, is stressed, snappy and can't get beyond constructing his revision timetable. Jay reveals his feelings for Chloe, but makes the mistake of asking his father for advice, and proceeds to stalk Chloe jealously by Facebook, text and Bebo. Simon abandons his own revision to help Carli, who lets slip that she's split from Tom – and gives him a lingering kiss. Will is wired on power drinks, and Jay says he's not allowed to revise because he has a photographic memory. The boys are headed for exam disaster – especially Will (Simon Bird, below). The power drinks take their toll, and as Will begs Mr Gilbert for leniency, he follows through, noisily, on a fart. Exams over, the others go to the pub to meet Chloe's mates. But Chloe tells Jay he's too needy for her, and Will turns up hours late, in lost-property tracksuit bottoms and with a bag holding his soiled clothes. Carli, of course, is back with Tom.

REPLAY MOMENT
Jay's personality inversion every time the boys say something crude about Chloe versus Will's "accident".

38

The School NEWSLETTER

SERIES 3 — read all about it!

3.1 FASHION SHOW

Angry: Simon blows it with Carli – again

A new school year at Rudge Park. Will failed his exams but Jay passed his driving test. He takes the boys to school in his mum's "mingemobile", and shows off his pierced left ear. Carli (Emily Head, above) has asked Simon to model in the school charity fashion show, but all Jay's efforts to wangle a strut up the runway fall flat. Former classmate Alastair Scott returns in a wheelchair – he had kidney failure, and the show is collecting for a dialysis machine. Neil and Jay say he was a dick even before he was ill. At the fashion show, Neil is dressing the (male) models and Mr Kennedy has his sights on Neil's trousers. When Charlotte arrives as a "special guest", Will has a strop with Alastair, wrapping him in a tablecloth so he can model with Charlotte. Carli begs Simon to help her out in her sexy feather boa routine. But it gets laughs, not adulation – not surprising, given that Simon has his bollock hanging out of his Speedos.

REPLAY MOMENT
Jay and Neil discussing the girls getting changed behind the curtain at the show – and failing to realize the girls can hear them.

3.2 THE GIG AND THE GIRLFRIEND

Jay is recounting one of his orgies – until his father says what a bullshitter he is. But Jay doesn't learn, it seems – next he's bragging about getting puff for the boys. Even Neil begins to wonder about Jay's tales. Simon runs after Carli into the common room – and falls into the lap of a girl in the year below. He and Tara (Hannah Tointon, below) get talking about music, and arrange to go to a gig. Simon asks Jay to score him some drugs, but all Mark Donovan will give Jay is tea in clingfilm. At the gig, Jay and Neil approach

Snog: Tara shows Simon her dinner

a young black guy they spot dealing and at last score some gear. Outside, the others pretend to be spliff pros, but Will refuses. Neil keels over from his cough syrup cocktail, Will, needled by Jay, necks the rest of the dope and Simon "Tony the Tiger" Cooper snogs Tara, who's just vomited. It all gets messy, as Will is overwhelmed by drug paranoia and is escorted into an ambulance.

REPLAY MOMENT
Tara's vom-and-snog with Simon. Ewww every time.

3.3 WILL'S DILEMMA

Outfit: Tara makes him look a twat

Neil's mum gives him a motorbike for his eighteenth birthday, but he can't ride it back from the showroom because he's broken his arm.

So on the basis that his dad had a drink with Lance Armstrong, Jay steps forward. Unfortunately, Jay is clueless and the bike gets trashed. Simon can't stop talking about Tara, and Jay beeps a "Tara alert". But Neil thinks it's a great idea to invite Tara and her fit mates to his birthday party. Simon drags Will into a double date with Tara's friend Kerry, who's apparently gorgeous – and gave her last three boyfriends blowjobs. At the mall, Tara flatters Simon (Joe Thomas, above) into buying a preposterous outfit, while Will discovers Amazonian Kerry is more on Neil's level in other ways, too. But there is the chance of sexual activity… At the end of the date, he can't quite let Kerry down, and lets her kiss him. But it all backfires at Neil's party. Will dumps Kerry (before any sex) only to discover her dad died recently – something Simon forgot to tell him. Will is hounded as a villain, but Neil does get an unexpected present.

❮❮❮❮❮ REPLAY MOMENT

Jay driving Neil's motorbike into the showroom wall.

3.4 A TRIP TO WARWICK

They've been going out for weeks, so Tara decides it's time she and Simon had sex. Simon panics and suggests the bushes at the bottom of the garden, but Tara says they can stay with her sister Sophie, who's at uni in Warwick. Simon foolishly accepts Jay and Neil's offer to come as moral support, and they all end up in the car to Warwick, Tara stuck grumpily in the back suffering Neil's McFarts. At Sophie's house, Will insults Warwick University and Jay mouths off about how filthy Dutch girls are. Neil and Jay get on brilliantly with Sophie's male housemate and his inane drinking-game

The real Warwick: Neil's uni choice

companions, who goad Will so much he eats a bonsai tree. Terrified he'll ejaculate too soon, Simon has a precautionary and unwise pre-wank, rendering him impotent, even when Tara kindly struggles to put a condom on with her mouth. Simon goes mental and shouts at his cock, Neil pisses everywhere but mostly on Will, in his sleep, Jay tries to have sex with Dutch girl Heike (see above), and they're all thrown out, without most of their clothes. Tara dumps Simon – by text.

❮❮❮❮❮ REPLAY MOMENT

Sophie's practical older-sisterly advice for Tara about losing her virginity, involving towels, a flannel and not enjoying it.

3.5 HOME ALONE

Jay's having trouble with dog Benjy – he won't leave Jay alone to have a wank. The boys are at Will's, encouraging his mum to bounce up and down to get the best from

Gutted: Will Jay ever wank again?

the Wii. She's about to go away for a weekend with Facebook friend Fergus, leaving Neil in charge of Will. But all the boys turn up and amuse themselves by kicking flowers in Will's neighbours' gardens and practising their golf swings (Simon has discovered he is quite good at golf, and has a tournament with his dad the next day). Jay takes on a poor squirrel in his mum's car on "pussy patrol", and the boys abuse Mrs McKenzie's Ocado account. Jay (James Buckley, above) still can't shake Benjy, and decides to say that the dog shat in the house, so he'll have to live in the garden. In the morning, the apoplectic neighbour whose flowers they destroyed lays siege to Will's house, with the boys trapped inside and Neil creating an appalling stench. Simon has missed the golf and his father's zillion messages, and Will floors an old lady when he kicks the door closed. Then Jay's father texts – he's had Benjy put down.

◄◄◄◄◄◄ REPLAY MOMENT
The squirrel incident – and Jay's instant remorse.

3.6 CAMPING

An emergency family meeting turns Simon's world upside down – they're moving to Swansea for his dad's job. Simon has an instant tantrum: his life is ruined, and that's it for him and Carli… Neil's had bad news, too. Though he did get some sex first. It looks like he has got a woman on the Asda cheese counter pregnant. Will announces they should go on a camping trip, then has to rescue a drunken Simon from breaking into Carli's house. The problem with Will's camping spot is that it's in the countryside, and the boys will have to dig their own toilet trenches –

Swansea: Does is mean the end?

or crap at the pub. They make a fire with Will's camping kit and some petrol, send texts on each other's phones, and try to use Simon's car headlamps as a light. But Jay has left the brake off, and they can't find the keys. Inevitably – well, not inevitably, but because Jay and Neil can't be bothered holding it any more – the car slides into the lake. There's truth, alcohol, bullshit, obscenities – and Neil's OK, because he just has an STD. Two *Inbetweeners* specials are planned, but is this really the final series?

◄◄◄◄◄◄ REPLAY MOMENT
Neil asking Jay about the games he used to play in the shed with his weird neighbour.

♪ THE INBETWEENERS THEME

The title track at the beginning of each episode is *Gone Up in Flames* (instrumental) by Morning Runner. The idea behind the name of the Reading band – who were together for four years in the mid-noughties – is that people who run in the morning are impressive for their efforts to better themselves.

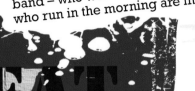

THAT FIRST EPISODE TRACK BY TRACK

* *Gallery* by Tellison (opening sequence with Will's introduction)
* *Foundations* by Kate Nash (walking down the corridor)
* *Love Is an Unfamiliar Name* by The Duke Spirit (Will ambushed by Donovan in the toilets)
* *Kill the Director* by Wombats (the photos of Will on the toilet)
* *Creepin up the Backstairs* by The Fratellis (school montage with Will)
* *Fill My Little World* by The Feeling (Will gets into his mum's car after school)
* *Fluorescent Adolescent* by Arctic Monkeys (the boys get ready to go out)
* *Song B* by Mumm-Ra (they go into the wrong pub)
* *SOS* by Rihanna (then finally make it to the right one)
* *Some Girls* by Rachel Stevens (the "under-age" showdown between Will and the bartender)
* *Dickhead* instrumental by Kate Nash (Will leaves the pub)
* *Don't Look Back into the Sun* by The Libertines (end credits)

For full track listings for each episode, see e4.com/inbetweeners.

BACK TO THE EIGHTIES

Set against New Wave-style graphics, the end tracks travel the musical range of the teens-to-thirties-plus audience, often seeming to link to teenagerdom, suburbia or the episode theme. So there's The Cure's *Inbetween Days*, The Jam's *That's Entertainment*, The Cribs' *Men's Needs* and The Maccabees' *Latchmere* ("Swimming, swimming…" after Simon's Swanage dip).

THE INBETWEENERS IN THE NME

The actors who play our four acne-heroes put on their Rudge Park ties for a day and went into the offices of the NME to do some "work experience". While there, they speculated on the musical tastes of their characters, as well as revealing the bands they're currently into themselves.

Will – Likes a bit of Radiohead, apart from the weird albums.

Simon – Something to fit his usually suicidal moods, such as Coldplay.

Jay – Marina (but not the Diamonds, obviously, because he's not bent).

Neil – More into R&B and bump and grind.

Simon Bird – Baltimore-raised experimental rockers Animal Collective.

Joe Thomas – Texas indie from Midlake.

James Buckley – New York psychedelics MGMT.

Blake Harrison – Plumstead's own Tinie Tempah.

JAY-WAY-SIS

James Buckley is an Oasis fan and has a tattoo of the Epiphone brand symbol (they're his hero Noel Gallagher's favourite guitars) on his wrist – though he gets stick because it looks like the euro currency sign. He also has "Live Forever" on his arm. Apparently, James has long been into the likes of Blur, The Stone Roses, The Smiths, Primal Scream and Paul Weller, and even joined Ocean Colour Scene's Steve Cradock on his new solo album. He likes rock, not synths, and used to play guitar in a Britpop-inspired band called London Waiting with fellow Essex boys. His dad taught him Lou Reed's *Perfect Day*. You might also catch James doing a DJ set now and then.

THE REAL BAND IN "THE GIG…"

In The Gig and the Girlfriend, Simon goes with Tara (and his mates, of course) to see real band Failsafe. The alt rockers from Preston are huge fans of the show – they used to play it on a laptop on their way to gigs.

ROCKIN

BIG

BEAT

Comin at ya!

School Drama Prize

Awarded to James Buckley (Jay)

The Essex boy enjoyed acting so much he went to weekend stage school from the age of seven. By the time he was eleven he was appearing in West End shows *Whistle Down the Wind* and *Les Misérables*.

He also turned up in an episode of *Teachers* in 2004 as John, a homosexual student who dresses as Freddie Mercury for Gay and Lesbian Awareness Week at Summerdown Comprehensive.

LOST PROPERTY

Items currently in the Lost Property box include:

- 1 pair of high-cut black Speedos (barely worn)
- 10 packets of out-of-date condoms – ribbed, strawberry flavour, etc
- Crowded House CD (case damaged, as though stamped on)
- Plastic bag containing Rizla papers and loose tea

PLEASE COME AND COLLECT IF THESE ARE YOURS!

Is this you...? Closet Inbetweeners fan gets caught out.

ABUSIVE LANGUAGE

Pupils are reminded that the term "bus wankers" is a form of abuse and should not be used under any circumstances.

As sixth-formers, we trust you to be ambassadors for the school, and uphold its values.

Fiat Hawaii's 4ever!

UNIVERSITY APPLICATIONS

Inbetweeners co-writer Damon Beesley has apparently always imagined that the show would finish at the end of the boys' final school year. After the summer holidays in the *Inbetweeners* film, he says they are going to disappear off to different universities.

Neil and Jay...? Studying for a degree...?

Damon added: **"It's very unlikely Neil is going to go to university."**

ZERO TOLERANCE FOR
VIOLENT BEHAVIOUR

At the age of seven Simon Bird (Will) asked a friend to punch him in the face, to see what it was like. His glasses got broken.

LONDON SOUTH WEST SCHOOLS
FOOTBALL LEAGUE

Milwaukee
Fried Chicken Trophy

Local posh school..... 32

Our team.................. 0

(One of our players sent home off the bench for offensive language.)

Fit girl 4 loser!

LOST: SCHOOL GOALPOSTS

When Joe Thomas (Simon) was growing up in Chelmsford, a story went round that a local character known as Mad Max had got into his school one night and stolen all the goalposts.

Morning, benders!

3

The hyper-talented cast

There they were, minding their own acting and stand-up business, and then along comes *The Inbetweeners*, and now they can barely cross the road without someone mistaking them for their characters.

The series has turned its cast into comedy icons. Even pin-ups (surely not... but we've got a poster of them in this book, so that must be true).

Find out how Simon Bird and Joe Thomas got spotted, where you've seen James Buckley before, why you should talk comics with Blake Harrison and who has a vomit phobia. Plus loads more about the Emilys, Hannah and Belinda – along with a fiendish exam paper (aka quiz) to test your *Inbetweeners* IQ.

Simon BIRD

Born: 19 August 1984 in Guildford, Surrey

Age: 26

Education: At the Royal Grammar School, Guildford, his class bought fruit every Friday lunchtime, then had a fruit fight in GCSE Biology. Studied English at Queen's College, Cambridge, then took an MA in Cultural and Critical Studies at Birkbeck College, London.

Family: Simon's father Graham is an economics professor at the University of Surrey. He called his family "the nutters" in his Best Comedy Actor acceptance speech.

Pre-tweeners career: House of Windsor, his comedy troupe with Joe Thomas and Jonny Sweet, appeared at the Edinburgh Fringe.

Fan of...

Marion and Geoff with Rob Brydon (which he was obsessed with at school), *Peep Show, The Office, The Thick of It,* 1990s US teen show *My So-Called Life.*

Other appearances: Hosted slightly bizarre comedy panel show *The King Is Dead* on BBC3 and also stars in Channel 4's *Friday Night Dinner*, written by *Inbetweeners* script editor Robert Popper. He and Joe Thomas have co-written and acted in First World War sitcom *Chickens* – they stay at home while everyone else is risking their lives on the Front.

Inside story: Simon Bird admits that he has Will-like geeky tendencies, and he's perhaps the actor most like his character. He and Joe Thomas got their roles partly through luck, and partly harassment. They were spotted by *Inbetweeners* creators Damon Beesley and Iain Morris at the Edinburgh Fringe, and did some writing for them. At first Beesley and Morris refused to audition the pair for the show, despite plenty of pestering – but the week before filming, they were frantic to find their leads for the series. Simon and Joe were hired.

Simon first got into drama when he took a year out to study at school in the US, where there was a big drama centre. When he returned to the UK he forced his school to let him do Drama A level.

He and Joe Thomas met while at Cambridge University, and in renowned student comedy group the Cambridge Footlights – which also spawned the Monty Python crew, Stephen Fry, and Mitchell and Webb.

Simon had never been on a rollercoaster before the Thorpe Park episode, and was so motion-sick they had to call a nurse. He swore to the others he'd never pass the entrance gates again, but had to come back the next week to re-do the scene because he'd looked too ill the first time.

Is he a Will with the girls?: Simon used to be seriously into corduroy, until girlfriend Lisa made him buy a new wardrobe.

Mind-numbing trivia

Simon Bird is a fully qualified football referee, and also colour blind. He has said he can't pee in public so has to use the cubicles.

JOE THOMAS

Born: 28 October 1983 in Chelmsford, Essex

Age: 27

Education: King Edward VI Grammar School in Chelmsford, where he got an A for his A level Theatre Studies. He was a History student at Pembroke College, Cambridge and has said that he became somewhat obsessed with his subject.

Family: His mother is reported to be an English teacher and his father a History lecturer at a sixth-form college.

Pre-tweeners career: Joe has been writing and performing comedy since he was seventeen, and was part of the Cambridge Footlights with Simon Bird. He acted, directed and wrote for several Footlights shows.

Other appearances: There is a rumour that he was part of Team TRACIE in the first series of *Robot Wars*. He has also voiced characters in *Dr Who* adaptations for radio.

Inside story: Filming *The Inbetweeners* has been like going to school and seeing all your mates, according to Joe Thomas. Apparently, he hasn't moved on from his teen years emotionally – he has said he still spends his time feeling sorry for himself and making serious mistakes.

When he's not acting in comedy, he's writing it. Joe teamed up with regular writing partner Jonny Sweet in 2003 at Cambridge University – where he also met Simon Bird. Joe says he was much too nervous to do stand-up on his own, so it was lucky that Jonny came along. You can spot Jonny in *Inbetweeners* series 3 in A Trip to London – he plays Dean, who comes between Will and his attempts to chat up Rachel.

Joe's biggest ambition is to be admired as a writer. And at least *Chickens*, the First World War sitcom he is co-writing and hopes to see on Channel 4, gives him a chance to use his History degree.

Joe also helped to promote the Vinspired awards, which recognize the charitable work done by young people. In an interview about them he admitted his worst ever chat-up line was: "Before I met you, all I could think about was History. Now all I can think about is you." (It didn't work.)

Is he a Simon with the girls?: Well… maybe… a bit… Joe Thomas has admitted he was once being given lots of little kisses on the lips by a girl at a party, but held off because he was terrified if he kissed a girl they'd be repulsed. But he did get together with Hannah Tointon – who as Tara shared a vom-snog with character Simon – in real life.

Mind-numbing trivia
Joe was still living at home with his parents after *The Inbetweeners* had become a success. He used to play football and was pretty good at the violin.

51

James BUCKLEY

Born: 14 August 1987 in Croydon, south London, then moved to Dagenham in Essex at the age of two

Age: 23

Education: Beam Primary School in Dagenham, then The Chafford School comprehensive in Rainham, Essex and Colins Performing Arts College in Romford.

Pre-tweeners career: James has been appearing in West End theatre shows from his early teens, followed by a string of primetime TV favourites including *Holby City*, *The Bill*, *Teachers* – and you can spot him in series 1, episode 7 of *Skins*, as Cassie's rehab boyfriend Simon. He was also in Johnny Vaughn's *'Orrible* and starred in an award-winning short film called *Veronique* (2002), as a boy who falls for a girl on the bus.

Fan of...

The Office, The Mighty Boosh and Steve Coogan, but what he would really like to be in is an episode of Peep Show.

Other appearances: You can't miss James as the young and cheeky Del Boy in *Rock and Chips*. As a huge fan of *Only Fools and Horses*, it was a dream when he had lunch one day with David Jason and Nicholas Lyndhurst – the original Del and Rodney. He's also in a music video for Brentwood band States of Emotion.

Inside story: James Buckley says he's nothing like Jay – apart from the time he suggested an orgy with his Twitter followers. He gets embarrassed at some of the lines, because he has to actually say them to real people. Especially the one in Field Trip, where he asks the old lady if she'll perform oral sex on him.

Music is an important part of James's life, he says, and the Gallagher brothers from Oasis have been role models. They came from nothing to make something of themselves, and that has given him faith in himself. He used to dress up in rock-star style, with sequinned silver scarves, but in recent years has kept more to jeans and T-shirts.

When he doesn't need to sport the highlighted Jay bowl cut, James likes to grow his hair as long as he can get away with. He was once in a cab with *Peep Show*'s David Mitchell, but was too scared to speak to him.

During his school days, James says he didn't learn a lot, but he did laugh. His comedy soulmate was Craig Johnson, who became a Rifleman in the army and was sadly killed on a training exercise.

Is he a Jay with the girls?: Absolutely not. The tabloids loved it when James Buckley started dating Scottish model Clair Meek, and photographers snapped their Caribbean holiday. She has described him as quiet, shy and thoughtful, and has said they aren't big party animals, but prefer a night in watching TV.

Mind-numbing trivia

Apart from himself, James Buckley's celebrity Soccer Six team would include Ronaldo, Wayne Rooney, John Terry, Fernando Torres and David Beckham.

BLAKE HARRISON

Born: 23 July 1985 in Greenwich, south-east London

Age: 25

Education: Trained at the BRIT School (at the same time as Leona Lewis and Katie Melua) and graduated from the East 15 Acting School in 2007.

Family: Blake's father was in the army, and after a time as a cabbie went on to join the Government Car and Despatch Agency, driving ministers around.

Pre-tweeners career: Blake enjoyed acting from primary school, and went to Saturday drama classes. At age ten he had a small part in *Oliver!* at the London Palladium. He acted in theatre productions at East 15, including Shakespeare's *Richard III*, and has also been in *The Bill*.

Other appearances: He was in the comedy drama film *Reuniting the Rubins*, starring Timothy Spall, and plays Dave in the sitcom *The Increasingly Poor Decisions of Todd Margaret*, which has been shown on US and UK TV.

Inside story: Blake has said that the lads got on really well, really quickly when they met on set. If he hadn't got the *Inbetweeners* job, he was about to start working in a charity call centre. Between series 1 and 2, he worked in the Scream chamber at Madame Tussauds – basically, he has said, lots of out-of-work actors in boiler suits and fake blood would jump out and scare people.

His most embarrassing moment was running around Thorpe Park in a pair of Speedos – in front of all the park visitors. One of his favourite lines from the show is whenever Neil's father, played by Alex MacQueen, says: "Oh, Neil!"

A fan of Millwall FC, Blake grew up in Peckham and says he spent all his time at school playing computer games. He wanted to be a superhero, and now collects classic comics such as *Batman* and *Nightwing*.

He has described himself as a hopeless romantic, and wouldn't have imagined he'd be playing a gormless character like Neil. Though he says he was very lucky to get the part just months after graduating from East 15.

Is he a Neil with the girls?: Like Neil, Blake has some wise advice about the opposite sex. Apparently, you should always listen to what a woman has to say – they don't like it if you forget what they've told you. Aged about fifteen, he was all set to go and ask out a girl he fancied, but ended up just tapping her on the shoulder and running away, because he was too scared.

Mind-numbing trivia
Blake is six feet one inch in height, but because the other *Inbetweeners* actors are shorter (James is five feet nine) people think he's taller than he is.

Emily HEAD

Born: 15 December 1988 in London

Age: 22

Education: Kingswood School, Bath, and the BRIT School – she was there a couple of years after Blake Harrison, so they didn't meet.

Family: Her father is Anthony Head, who's probably best known for playing Rupert Giles in *Buffy the Vampire Slayer* and the fictional prime minister in *Little Britain*. Emily's mother, Sarah Fisher, works with dogs and horses, and helps to train dogs for disabled people. Her younger sister, Daisy, is also an actor.

Pre-tweeners career: Emily first trained as a dancer and has appeared in plenty of dance and theatre shows. She went straight from sixth form into acting.

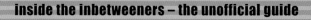

Other appearances: You may have caught her in *MI High*, *Doc Martin*, *Trial and Retribution* or *Doctors*. She also appeared with Noel Fielding in indie horror comedy *I Spit on Your Rave*. The film got into *Guinness World Records* for having the most zombies ever caught on camera – filmed at the Big Chill festival.

Inside story: Emily Head says that she and Emily Atack (who plays Charlotte) held their own on the boysy *Inbetweeners* set. The male actors are more gentlemanly than their characters – or some of them are, according to Emily.

She has admitted that she has no idea what the text Carli sent to Simon at the end of series 3 actually said (remember, the one after the boys swapped mobiles...), but she thinks that the show's writers do – so perhaps we'll all find out in the *Inbetweeners* film.

Emily's parents have a farm in Somerset. She went to secondary school in nearby Bath, where she appeared in plays and musicals, and trained at the Dorothy Coleburne School of Dancing. When her father was in *Buffy*, Emily went over to school in Los Angeles for a while. On the US set, she says, there was a massive table of food available all day – whereas in the UK, it seems actors have to wait around for a plate of sandwiches and cake.

She appeared with her father in comedy crime drama *The Invisibles*, as Grace Riley – the daughter of his character. But apparently the producers didn't know she was Anthony's real-life daughter when they called her in to audition.

Emily turned down the opportunity to appear in *Dancing on Ice*, but was a big supporter of *Inbetweeners* friend Emily Atack.

Mind-numbing trivia
Emily has never dieted, as she loves eating pizza too much, but she does walk everywhere.

57

EMILY ATACK

Other appearances: *Dancing on Ice* – the TV show and the tour. She was in the original *Rock and Chips*, with James Buckley.

Inside story: Emily has said that she would probably be friends with Charlotte if they were at school together: Charlotte is flirty and popular, but likeable rather than a bitch. Emily has also admitted she can be a bit flirty herself.

She revealed that she had been badly bullied at her own school because of her famous relatives. But, she has said, her tight-knit family really supported her and rather than being seen as a victim, it made her stronger.

In early 2010 Emily took part in *Dancing on Ice*, paired with US pro skater Fred Palascak. They lost out in a skate-off in week eight, and a tearful Emily said she didn't know what she was going to do with herself now the skating was over.

Born: 18 December 1989 in Ampthill, Bedfordshire

Age: 21

Family: Daughter of actress and singer Kate Robbins and musician Keith Atack. Sir Paul McCartney is a cousin and she knows him as Uncle Paul.

Pre-tweeners career: Emily managed to get an agent at age seventeen and her first TV appearance was *Blue Murder*, with Caroline Quentin.

Fan of...
The Office, Extras and EastEnders. Apparently her favourite quote is David Brent saying: "El vino did flow."

Mind-numbing trivia
Mother Kate Robbins has appeared in the *Eurovision Song Contest*, TV series *Dinnerladies* and *Sex Lives of the Potato Men* with Johnny Vegas, and voiced characters on the *Discworld* computer games.

Hannah TOINTON

Born: 28 December 1987 in Essex

Age: 23

Family: Hannah's older sister is *EastEnders* star and *Strictly Come Dancing* winner Kara Tointon. They grew up in Leigh-on-Sea.

Pre-tweeners career: Hannah was in *Whistle Down the Wind* in the West End in 2000. Her first TV role was in CBBC sitcom *Kerching!*.

Other appearances: *Hollyoaks* – of course!

Inside story: Hannah has said that she never laughed so much reading something as when she first got the *Inbetweeners* script. She watched the whole of series 1 and 2 in a night and became an instant fan.

Hannah's family weren't theatrical (father Ken is an accountant), but when Kara found an agent and started to get roles, Hannah followed in her footsteps. She and Kara have both taken TV scripts home to practise with their dad. Hannah has also admitted to raiding her big sister's wardrobe – but it can cause arguments when she customises Kara's clothes by cutting the arms off.

In *Hollyoaks*, Hannah played Katy Fox, Warren's younger sister, who became caught up in a love triangle. She had decided at the start that she would only do the show for a year.

Mind-numbing trivia

Hannah has a vomit phobia, and even pretending to be sick makes her feel sick. So that scene with Tara and Simon at the gig wasn't her favourite…

BELINDA STEWART-WILSON

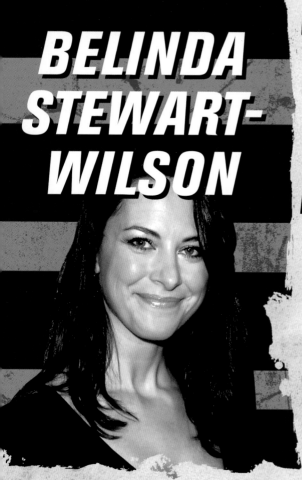

Born: 16 April 1970 in London

Age: 42

Family: Her father, Sir Blair Stewart-Wilson, was in the army and later an equerry to the Queen. Married comedian and actor Ben Miller in 2004. They have a son, Sonny, but are now separated.

Pre-tweeners career: She trained at the Webber Douglas Academy of Dramatic Art in London. Her first role was in 1995, in *Shine On Harvey Moon*, later followed by a part in *Goodnight Sweetheart*.

Other appearances: Comedies such as *Look Around You* and *The IT Crowd*. She was baddie Christine Johnson in series 3 of *Primeval* and plays Stinky in comedy hit *Miranda*. Other TV and films include *Joe's Palace* with Michael Gambon and sketch shows with Bremner, Bird and Fortune and Peter Serafinowicz.

Inside story: Belinda has said she nearly turned down the role of Mrs McKenzie, because she was worried she was too young to play a sixth-former's mother. In the read-through for series 3 she was blushing all the time, because of the filthy things the boys had to say about her.

She has always been into comedy. When she was young, Belinda has said, she had a squint and a patch over one eye, so would try to make people laugh to get them on her side. But she thought her patch was quite cool – like a pirate. At age eight she used to put on comedy sketches at her boarding school.

In *Primeval*, Belinda co-starred with husband Ben Miller – as his character's boss. It sounds as though she rather enjoyed that part of her role.

Irish band Pugwash wrote a song for their new album dedicated to her and entitled *Dear Belinda*.

Mind-numbing trivia
Belinda drives her dad's old green Rover, and has said it's like a skip inside. Her first and favourite car was a Mini Mayfair, but she'd like an Aston Martin DB7 Vantage.

which inbetweener girl are you like? (or are you will's mum?)

1. What's your idea of a fabulous evening out?
a) Sparkling wine and lively conversation with someone kind, funny and skilled in the bedroom.
b) An amazing gig with loads of moshing, then a sweet but drunken snog.
c) Clubbing in London with your older boyfriend.
d) You don't get many evenings out – being a mother is so demanding.

2. Who's your fantasy man?
a) Who needs fantasies when there are so many real men to play with?
b) Kurt Cobain. When he was alive, of course.
c) Stuart Broad – someone sporty, good-looking and high-achieving.
d) Well, there was this French... Oh, you mean men my own age?

3. What would make you dump your boyfriend?
a) Him lying about what the two of you got up to.
b) If he threw up on you...? No – you're capable of grossness yourself. But if he went all weird...
c) Him ignoring you – and going out with his mates.
d) Unfortunately you don't always get to do the dumping – the selfish gits.

4. How do you reckon boys think about you?
a) They're usually too blinded by lust to realize you've got a brain. More's the pity.
b) Like you care! But come to think of it, now you've got good hair and a bigger rack, you have had more attention...
c) They respect you – except for the immature ones, and you're not interested in what they think.
d) Boys? Think about me? Like that...?

so who are you?

Mostly a)
You're quite a grown-up compared with the males around you. Perhaps the curvy, knowing Charlotte would be your role model.

Mostly b)
Up for adventure and into your music – maybe you'd be a mate of Tara's. Although you may want to watch whose feet you're throwing up over.

Mostly c)
Ambitious, attractive and one of the popular girls – you want to be mature and at the centre of things. Just don't be too mean to your "Simon".

Mostly d)
Yes, there are women over thirty who love *The Inbetweeners*. But maybe not dwell on what your son's friends are fantasizing.

Exam time...!

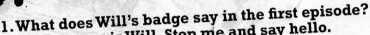

No, not really, but there'll be detention for anyone found cheating.

1. What does Will's badge say in the first episode?
   a) My name is Will. Stop me and say hello.
   b) My name is Will. But you can call me Briefcase Wanker.
   c) My name is Will, and I'm pretty sure I'm cleverer than you.

2. What is Will and Simon's excuse for Will's tirade at Neil's father and Simon's vomiting spree?
   a) They thought they were drinking cough medicine.
   b) Mark Donovan force-fed them bottles of whisky.
   c) Neil's father touched them – here, and here, and here (indicated on a doll).

3. What's the worst thing about Simon's car?
   a) It's yellow.
   b) It has a tape deck.
   c) The back seats are always damp and smell of piss and/or farts.

4. Why did Will wear a wig on his date with Daisy, his old babysitter?
   a) To disguise a bad haircut from his mum.
   b) Daisy once professed a fetish for really curly hair on a man.
   c) He'd gone bald "downstairs".

5. Why did Chloe dump Jay in series 2?
   a) She had too much schoolwork to have time for a relationship.
   b) He was too sensitive and intense for her.
   c) His penis was too big.

6. Which of these was Will *not* called after his exam room incident?
   a) Brad Shit.
   b) The Sheriff of Shittingham.
   c) Vladimir Pootin.

7. What is Simon's hair compared to in Fashion Show in series 3?
    a) Pete Doherty's toilet brush.
    b) The Statue of Liberty.
    c) A ferret that's been spunked on.

8. Why does Carli suddenly call on Simon to do the fashion show finale with her?
    a) Her modelling partner got drunk and passed out in the toilets.
    b) Jay's pierced ear got infected, so he couldn't do it.
    c) Her original partner's back looks like when you get hair caught in the plughole.

9. Which of these do the boys *not* suggest putting the supposed "puff" in when they can't roll a joint before the Failsafe gig?
    a) Hot chocolate.
    b) Jelly.
    c) Egg on toast.

10. When did Jay lose his virginity?
    a) With three girls over the table in his parents' caravan.
    b) When he was nine, with a fit babysitter.
    c) With a filthy Dutch girl.

ANSWERS

1. a) 2. c) 3. All of these, of course – but b) is what sends Simon over the edge when he first sees his little Fiat Cinquecento Hawaii. 4. c) 5. b) – but c) according to Jay. 6. b) 7. b) 8. c) 9. a) 10. None of these, as Jay is still a virgin at the end of series 3.

Written and edited by:
Charlotte Wilson for Harris + Wilson

Creative design and illustration:
Paul Cherrill for Basement68

Editorial direction: Emily Thomas

Picture research: Josine Meijer

PHOTOGRAPHIC ACKNOWLEDGEMENTS:
Getty Images: 1 above right, below left and centre, 2, 25, 26, 27, 32, 38, 40, 43, 48, 50, 56. Press Association: 7, 9, 11, 13, 15, 41 left. Rex Features: 1 above left and centre, below right, 6, 8, 10, 12, 14, 16, 17, 18, 19, 20, 21, 22, 23, 24, 30, 33, 34 right, 35, 39, 52, 54, 58, 59, 60, 61. Shutterstock: 32 left, 34 left, 36, 37, 40 right, 41 right.

Images used throughout for creative graphics: iStockphoto, Shutterstock.

Additional photography: Paul Cherrill.

Text copyright © Hodder and Stoughton Ltd 2011

Published in hardback in 2011 by Hodder and Stoughton Ltd, a division of Hachette Livre UK. The right of Charlotte Wilson to be identified as the Author of this Work has been asserted by her in accordance with the Copyright, Designs and Patents Act 1988

1

A Catalogue record for this book is available from the British Library

ISBN: 978 1 444 90461 1

Printed in Italy

Hodder and Stoughton Ltd
Hachette Livre UK
338 Euston Road, London NW1 3BH

The End